THE SLEEPERS IN THE CAVE

Quran Stories for Little Hearts

SANIYASNAIN KHAN

ILLUSTRATED BY MANAB BHATACHARYA

Goodword Books Pvt. Ltd.
1, Nizamuddin West Market
New Delhi-110 013
Tel. 435 6666, 435 5454
Fax 9111-435 7333, 435 7980
e-mail: info@goodwordbooks.com
Website: www.goodwordbooks.com

Goodwordkidz

Helping you build a family of faith

First published 2003
© Goodword Books 2003

It was about A.D. 250, during the rule of a Roman King Decius (Daqyanus), that the teachings of the Prophet Isa (Jesus)  were spread throughout the region by his early followers.

The people there were idol worshippers and the
moon was treated as a god and worshipped. But
seven young men of a noble family accepted the new
religion in Ephesus, an ancient city near the western
coast of Turkey, whose ruins can still be seen.
Decius took up arms against the new converts.

Due to their fearless preaching and willingness to give up everything so as to tread the right path, they were honored with the high status of being near to Allah.

When these young believers realized that the king's soldiers were about to capture them, they ran away from the town. They took refuge in a cave so as to escape the cruelty of the king.

As they ran, they prayed to Allah: "Our Lord! show us Your Mercy and save our lives!" They ran far into the wilderness, until they found a dark cave.

They entered in it with great caution, and hoped that no one would guess that there was anyone inside. Then weeping, they all prayed to Allah for His help.

8

9

Allah heard their prayers and, when they lay down to rest, He caused a miracle to happen. With His supreme power over life and death, He made them fall into a deep sleep lasting 200 years. Not once during this time did they awaken. They neither ate nor drank nor made any sound.

They only turned from side to side in their sleep. Even their dog Qitmir joined them in their long slumber with his legs stretched out across the entrance to the cave. This cave was so placed that not even a ray of light could enter it. Allah had also made it look so frightening that, if anyone had come close to it, he would have felt afraid and run away. It was one of the wonders of Allah.

13

Time passed and the town they had left changed altogether. The cruel king had died and the present king had become a believer, a follower of the message of Isa عليه السلام. The king and the people were believers in Allah and were no longer idol-worshippers. During this period, Allah woke up the sleeping men. As they arose up from their long slumber and stretched their arms and legs, one of them wondered, "How long have we been here?"

They thought about it, then said, "We have been here for a day or part of a day." They did not realize that they had been sleeping there for more than two centuries! They felt very hungry, so one of them crept out of the cave to fetch something to eat. He reached the town and went to a shop to buy some food. He paid the shopkeeper with a silver coin.

The shopkeeper was amazed to see such an old coin and suspected that this man might have found some old hidden treasure. So he took him to the king, who immediately recognized that he must be one of those men who had been lost for more than two hundred years.

19

By order of the king, the date they were lost their names and other particulars had been engraved on a lead slab which was kept in the Royal Treasury. For this reason they also came to be known as the "men of the slab." When the slab was taken out, it was confirmed that these were the very men who had run away from the city to save their lives more than two centuries ago.

They immediately became the centre of people's devotion. The new Roman King, Theodosus, himself went on foot to see them and seek their blessings. When these young men died, a place of worship was built at their cave as a memorial.

23

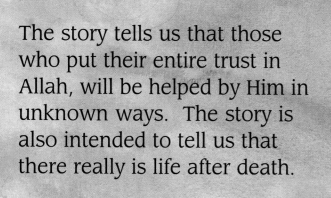

The story tells us that those who put their entire trust in Allah, will be helped by Him in unknown ways. The story is also intended to tell us that there really is life after death.

Find Out More

To know more about the message and meaning of Allah's words, look up the following parts of the Quran which tell the story of King Dhul Qarnayan.

Surah al-Kahf 18:10-21

علیه السلام *Alayhis Salam* 'May peace be upon him.' The customary blessings on the prophets.